GLENN THOMAS

plan b sucks!

a guide to unlocking your gifts
and living your authentic life

The caged bird sings
with a fearful trill
of things unknown
but longed for still
and his tune is heard
on the distant hill
for the caged bird
sings of freedom

- Dr. Maya Angelou[1]

---

[1] Angelou, M. (1969) I know Why The Caged Bird Sings. Random House.

This publication is designed to provide accurate and authoritative information in regard to the subject matter covered. It is sold with the understanding that neither the author nor the publisher is engaged in rendering legal, accounting, securities trading, or other professional services. If legal advice or other expert assistance is required, the services of a competent professional person should be sought.

From a Declaration of principles Jointly Adopted by a Committee of the American Bar Association and a Committee of Publishers and Associations.

Library of Congress Cataloging-in-Publication Data

Publisher: Heart Work Books & Publishing, LLC
support@glennathomas.com

Design by: ALYN, https://www.alynmarketinggroup.com

ISBN: 978-0-578-24834-9

DEDICATION

This book is dedicated to Ishna Hall.
A phenomenal woman of Delta Sigma Theta Sorority, Incorporated: a daughter, sister, auntie, friend, servant leader, coach, connector, academic, and every adjective that describes what it means to simply be EXTRAORDINARY.

We love you. We miss you. We will never forget you.

TABLE OF CONTENTS

INTRODUCTION

Plan B Sucks!

. . . .

To all the caged birds: live free. - Glenn

When I was a kid, I vividly remember my mother being very clear about her personal beliefs on life. One of those beliefs was that one should always play to win. No matter what the game was, my mom insisted that winning should be the number one goal. And let's be clear, even if I was in a school yard fight, my mother was adamant that I could not even think about coming home if I had let some kid get the best of me.   It was either win or lie about losing; but it couldn't be anything in between.

We didn't have participation trophies or consolation prizes; you either won or you lost. The coach never said, "If you can't win, then lose." That sounds just as ridiculous as having a plan-B! So no, I didn't grow up with this notion that if you didn't achieve your initial goal, then you should tap into your back-up plan. It wasn't until I was in college and planning on what was going to come next in my life, did people begin to plant the seed of this plan-B mindset.

It makes you think - if achieving your goals in life is so important, then why is it when it comes to your most passionate aspirations, young adults are taught to always have a plan-B? It just doesn't make any sense. Growing up, I was taught, like so many people I know, (in my Coach Herman Edwards voice) that you play to win the game. You want to be 1st chair in band? Then practice your butt off so you can win your seat. You want to make the tennis team? Then get up at 5AM everyday so you can be the first on the court and make sure you are the last to leave. You want to get a college scholarship? Then push yourself to make "A's"so you can go to any school you choose.

But never did I hear, just do good enough to get by and maybe you will win 1st chair; or just practice when you can and they may see that you have potential; or just study most nights and you will at least receive a partial scholarship to a school.

Nope. I never heard that reasoning when it came to school or extra-curricular activities; I never even heard it when it came to having a crush on a girl. My mom would say, "Go talk to the girl you like, son; the worst thing that can happen is that she will say no."

So if this attitude of "going for it" was the guiding principle of living life, why in the world did it change after we turned 18? The entire idea of doing our best was based on a premise that if there was a goal, a desire, and a destination, then we would go hard for it. Yet, that attitude of fortitude was shamefully cast aside when the question was, "What do you want to do with your life?" Yes, that infamous question that we all have had the pleasure of hearing on more than one occasion.

So many of us would say, "I want to be a doctor, a lawyer, or a teacher." But what about those of us who wanted to be artists, rappers, gamers, or writers? Seemingly, those of us who didn't fall within the parameters of the "good job" status would certainly need a plan-B...just in case of course. Or maybe being a lawyer was also a stretch because we may not have had the grades that demonstrated our ability to compete in the rigor of law school; so a plan-B was a necessary option in order to play it safe, with a likely and probable failed plan-A.

I don't ever recall waking up and having this burning desire to be second fiddle to anything. I always wanted to win, and losing was not something that was even an option to me. As a kid, did you ever say to yourself, "I just want to be second. That would be amazing!" Not ever! You didn't have a plan-B, and neither did I. Now, if you had a different upbringing, I get it; and I'm still talking to you, so don't abandon this book yet.

As I look around, I see so many people working their plan-B, or even worse, their plan-C. And I mean they are working the hell out those backup plans. Those are the plans that were chosen because plan-A didn't pan out the way that you wanted it to. So plan-B was just sitting there, waiting, hoping that you would just take second place, knowing that once you succumbed to plan-B, plan-A would become a distant memory.

Is that where you are? Are you working someone else's plan-A? And, at the same time, are you kicking yourself because you thought that plan-B's were a great idea, until you realized that it's just a politically correct way of saying "I give up."

When we intentionally create a plan-B, we are consciously telling ourselves that if plan-A fails, I have another option. But what we are really saying to ourselves is that **when** plan-A fails, I have plan-B to fall back on.

Fall back? Who in the hell wants to fall back? Denzel Washington said it best, "We should fall forward." And he hit it on the mark. If you want to fall back, then why even have a dream in the first place. Plan-B and plan-C are easy!

I decided to write this book for the people out there who find themselves living someone else's plan-A; not their plan, but a plan that was built by someone else, for someone else. If this story pertains to you, then you are in the right place. I am not pulling any punches in this book. I'm not trying to be applauded or receive accolades for writing a "*how to*" book. I am driven to fight for all the dreamers and fighters in the world who desire to   live out their plan-A. **Why? Because plan-B sucks!**

This isn't rocket science; it's really simpler than that. We have been trained in this mindset that having a plan-B will provide us financial and professional security in life. My God, that's so much bull-crap I can hardly keep down my lunch just typing it.

An excerpt from my first book "Heart Work," shares my theory on why we must have a growth mindset to focus on our plan-A:

When you carry around a fixed mindset you are effectively fighting yourself. Yes, we all think about 'what if' when it comes to the important things in our life, especially our careers and families. But if you invested your energy into what you are passionate about, and not your plan-B, your outcomes would be drastically different. Well, what happens when my plan-A fails Glenn? If you are determined and believe in what you want out of life, then pick up those pieces and find another way. What I have learned from all of these gutsy moments was that I was so busy worrying about what wouldn't work (and what didn't work), I wasn't spending time on what I wanted to work. See the difference...I was opting out of everything that wasn't easy - including my marriage. Why? Because I had a plan-B.

My attitude was not constructed with a plan-A-only growth mindset; an attitude that challenged me to put in the necessary work so that I could achieve my audacious goals in life. So I had to check myself, check my mindset and choose to shift my attitude to receive the blessings that were right in front of me. Now, ask yourself, what type of mindset are you leading with? [2]

---

[2] Thomas, G. (2020) Heart Work: 19 Expressions of Heart-Centered Leaders. Heart Work Books & Publishing.

1. NOT A DRESS REHEARSAL

Wakeup every day as if you only get one take

. . . .

I decided that the pain that I was feeling in my right arm was beginning to be too much for me to handle. I knew I needed to call the doctor to find out what was going on. The pain had been with me for years and I'd never really addressed it. But in the moment where I was feeling as though I had no choice but to call the doctor, I realized something - I was scared. That fear, that feeling of smallness and helplessness was centered in my stomach. I wasn't Superman anymore. I couldn't leap tall buildings in a single bound (you get the picture). I knew in that moment I would have to face the fear that I had not admitted to myself. I was scared of not being "here" anymore. Mortality just became real.

As I sat in the doctor's office and tried to keep my mind on something other than what was about to take place, I attempted to laugh off the reasons why it took me so long to follow through on my appointment. I had rescheduled enough times to where I had to receive constant reminders to follow up with the doctor. I didn't think much of it. The pain had come and gone, and I figured, "What the hell, it couldn't be that bad, right?"

Just a few months earlier, a family friend had passed away in her sleep. Barely forty years of age, she was no longer with us and it literally rocked our family's world. The questions were endless. How did it happen? What could we have done? The questions that we just didn't have answers to, and honestly, they seemed minor in comparison to the loss that had tragically imploded our lives. And as I sat in the doctor's office reflecting on her not being with us anymore, I had my first awakening moment of clarity. One day, I would be the person not waking up. One day, I won't be here and what will that mean?

So there I was, sitting, trying to act as if I had no worries in the world. But I knew the truth. The receptionist knew the truth. She could see it in my demeanor, I'm sure. And yeah, I tried to treat it as any other moment...the moment where I had control of everything, when in reality, I had none.

When the doctor stepped out, she called my name and I remember the heart sinking feeling I felt. Because this felt like the moment that I would find out my life has an expiration date. And the uniqueness of this expiration date was that I would know the exact date (sorta kinda). Yeah, I know it sounds kind of hyperbolic, but we all know that we will die. But when you find yourself about to be diagnosed with an illness that has close to a 100% success rate, it's just a little bit different type of feeling.

As I was walking through the hallway, I recalled the feeling of seeing my grandfather thirty years ago in the hospital when he was close to the end of his life. And here I was, trying to shrug off this moment of intense fear, thinking about all the things I had done, all the things I wanted to do. In that moment, in that hallway, I felt as hopeless as I have ever felt before.

Once inside the room, I jumped on the table as the nurse came in to give me instructions that literally went in one ear and out the other. I could see her lips moving and I could see her expression in her face, but I literally heard nothing she was saying. I knew that moment was about to change my life forever; I just didn't know exactly how. They didn't know and I didn't know.   It was just a moment that had to happen for me to take another step towards my fear.

After playing x-ray gymnastics for about 30 minutes, I was ready to get the hell up out of the doctor's office. The best they could tell me was that they would review the x-rays and would let me know what they found.   I really wanted to just tell her that's not good enough. I mean, my life is in your hands right now and the unknown would weigh too much on me, and I just didn't know what to do with myself.

But unfortunately or fortunately, I had no choice. So I waited, and eventually the call came from the doctor to come back in to sit with her to discuss what they saw on the x-rays.   I remember thinking to myself after the call, "Couldn't they just tell me on the phone?" I feared that it must be so bad that they need me to be there just in case I have an emotional breakdown. I began doing things like checking on my life insurance to make sure there was enough coverage to take care of bills and family for a reasonable period of time after I was gone. I literally had come to a place where I was counting down the days (I was probably being a tad bit over dramatic , but I'm trying to paint a vivid picture of how I was really feeling).

I was back in the doctor's office again for the second time now, and there was no one around. I was the only patient there waiting. And again, I surmised that they scheduled me early so that if anything happened while they were breaking this life altering news to me, they wouldn't have to calm down any other patients. I was mentally getting prepared, reflecting on all the good things I'd done in life, all the fun times I had, all the learning experiences that mattered to me and helped me be a better person.

To say that I had gone into a place of panic would be an understatement. I was so beyond panic that it didn't even matter to me anymore. So I walked into the room and she began with the typical general conversation, asking me how I felt and had I experienced the pain anymore. But again, I wondered why they just wouldn't get to the point. Why wouldn't they tell me what they saw? But I guess she was just trying out her bedside manner.

Finally, she reached for the folders with the x-rays; I had seen them when I first walked in the room and hadn't taken my eyes off them the entire time. I had to brace myself because my heart was beating faster than any time in my life, other than the time that I was witnessing my first child being born into the world. But this was definitely a different type of heartbeat. This heartbeat was that of pure, unadulterated fear and anxiety. And then the doctor began to speak.

"We don't see anything that stands out in your arm and neck," she said to me. "So right now, we believe that we need to do MRIs because based on your symptoms, there's a possibility you may have multiple sclerosis (MS)[3]." When she said those words, I thought to myself, "Did she just say multiple sclerosis?" She continued to speak in reference to a previous patient who was similar to me in age and symptoms, and had been diagnosed with MS in weeks prior. In my mind I was thinking, "What in the hell is the doctor talking about?" And I really wanted to use more colorful and direct words of a different nature.

Through all of my worry and concern about my life, I had not ever thought about MS. Even though some close friends had suggested to me MS sounded like the symptoms I was experiencing, I tried to dismiss that thought for

---

[3] Multiple Sclerosis is a potentially disabling disease of the brain and spinal cord (central nervous system)

some reason. I just wanted it to be something else. There was no cure for this, and I wasn't ready for that discussion. My fear quickly turned into dread.

The nonchalant manner in which she told me that she would set up my appointment for my MRI did not sit well with me. I pondered if I should be upset that she so cavalierly suggested I was possibly stricken with MS. Or should I have been happy that she was forthright enough to be able to try to exclude what, I believed, would be a life altering diagnosis for me? Either way, I was leaving that office not knowing what my life would be like that day forward.

I jumped in my car and the first thing I thought was I need a drink. The only problem was I had recently stopped drinking. I laughed at the fact that, here I am about to find out that I have an expiration date, I don't drink any more, and life in this moment just sucks. Where was a Jack Daniels with ginger when you needed one? After getting back home, I didn't immediately say anything to anyone about it. I needed more time to think. I needed more time to process what I was feeling before I shared what was about to take place.

The MRI date was coming quickly, and after rescheduling twice, I finally followed through with my appointment. While waiting on my name to be called, what should have been a thirty minute wait, turned into two hours of brutal torture…two hours of sitting in the hospital contemplating what was about to happen. I fixed my eyes on patients and their families coming in and leaving. I thought about what they were experiencing; were they there for something life-threatening, or did they not know yet what was happening inside of their bodies? I began to feel empathy and sadness for them. As I sat in that cold plastic chair, I was examining the life I remembered and the life that I never chose to live.

Life has a way of being funny sometimes, and in those moments, waiting past the time I was supposed to wait, I was able to do some soul-searching. As I was looking at the people coming in and out of the hospital, I realized that people get sick, and people die. My wife had just lost her best friend in the world without any notice. And here I was about to have the *blessing of notice*.

Right then and there, I literally slapped myself in the face and said, "Wake the f@%$ up!" What was I doing? Why had I already given up while I still had breath in my lungs? I had fallen into a state of selfishness and pity, and I had not realized the blessing that was sitting right smack dab in front of me. I had received *notice*.   I had just been given the opportunity to see that life was not, in any way, a certainty.

Here I was, with an unknown number of days ahead of me, just like everyone else in the world. *And the real reason I was fearful wasn't that I feared dying - I was ashamed because I feared living.*

As I laid inside that MRI machine for almost an hour of time, the noise was so loud that it pushed me to my limits. I had to trick my mind into thinking that this was a brainstorming session and that I would figure out all the ways my mind needed to shift, all the things that I wanted to do, in order to live my life to the fullest with no regrets.

So here I was trying to figure out what I would do next. My reality was that I had thought that nothing could happen to me, even though I knew that one day I would eventually die. Now I was hit with the stark reality that this could be a moment that would literally change the rest of my life. And so it was…I was lost in my own silence.

I walked out of the hospital annoyed that I would have to straighten up; I would have to literally figure some things out about myself, my strength, and my courage; and in areas of my life that I had never challenged myself on before. But there was a sense of calm as I walked through the parking lot. There were ducks walking around in the parking lot, making noises and having fun, doing what ducks do. And it dawned on me that there I was in the midst of a storm, and the ducks were just having fun.

What was I scared of? Was it that I was going to miss my kids growing up or miss all the things I enjoyed doing in life? Or was I actually just really sad that I had not done all the things that I had always dreamed of doing? Was I really in a place of joy in my life? And I guarantee in that moment I realized it wasn't anger that I was feeling. In that moment, I realized I was sad because I was in a place of understanding reality; leaving this world and not living out the dreams and ambitions I had always had in my heart. In that moment, I was shaken.

So the only answer, the only thing that I could do in that moment, was to actually take back control of my life - my destiny. Was I going to die? Yeah. When was it going to happen? The hell if I knew. But, what I did know was as long as I had breath in my body, I needed to take a hard look at my mindset about my life. I had always considered myself to have a very level head about how to live my purpose in life and all the things that kind of go along with being conscious and being present in the world.

I knew then, what I live now. There are moments that change you, and there are moments that are life changing. I was experiencing both.

So I gave myself the best pep talk I could ever give. I said, *"Glenn, Get your butt up and start living. Get off the sidelines watching others; be a star in your life. This isn't a dress rehearsal and the movie is happening with or without you. You've been sitting here dreaming, so it's time to start doing and start living. Glenn, you may not receive notice again, so it's best that you begin waking up with purpose, on purpose, and live your best life. Did you hear me? Are you living in your purpose? Glenn, I need you to live the words that you speak every single morning. Begin every day with gratitude. Extend at least one act of unconditional kindness every single day. It's a yes to more. And more doesn't mean more stuff. More means more of the abundance of joy and fulfillment that God has in store for you. Glenn, I need you to believe in what God has already planned for your life…go be great!".*

If my pep talk to myself resonates with you at all, then you are in the right space, at the right time, experiencing the right moment. Keep reading and I promise you that you will begin to understand more clearly why plan-B really does suck!

2. STOP PLAYING SMALL

You're bigger than that

. . . .

Life can feel so complex. From learning what the world pur-
ports as success, to hearing your parents and friends tell you
what you should do in your life. The fact is, no one knows
what your life should look like, other than you. But, if you
wish to live a so-called "safe" life, a life with less chances of
failure - you have chosen to play small. And if that is you,
there is no shame in your choice; but we all must recognize
that playing small is, in fact, a choice. Playing it small is not
what God intended for your life. Proverbs 18:16 really
speaks volumes on just how meaningful your purpose is in

this world: "A mans gift makes room for him." My question to you is, "Are you using your gifts? "

People in the world are asking more often now, "What is my purpose in life?" The truth is, purpose is not static. It can change, evolve, or reset. The issue I see more often than not is that people don't have an idea of what their purpose is. The challenge is, so many people allow their circumstances or other people define *what* their purpose is. We get led into believing that we would be better off by going down the "practical" path - whatever that means.   Our minds begin to play tricks on us because we followed the "small" play, leaning towards our bank account, and not our purpose.

But why is this the story of so many people in the world? Most people would agree that the world is mostly full of caring people. So if so much of the world actually cares for others, why encourage this mindset of settling - this imaginary construct of "playing small"?

at makes us so uncomfortable when consider-
d created us to be? Author and political activist
Villiamson says it best in her acclaimed best sell-
ing book, *A Return to Love*:

> *Our deepest fear is not that we are inadequate. Our deepest fear is that we are powerful beyond measure. It is our light, not our darkness that most frightens us. We ask ourselves, 'Who am I to be brilliant, gorgeous, talented, fabulous?' Actually, who are you not to be? You are a child of God. Your playing small does not serve the world. There is nothing enlightened about shrinking so that other people won't feel insecure around you. We are all meant to shine, as children do. We were born to make manifest the glory of God that is within us. It's not just in some of us; it's in everyone. And as we let our own light shine, we unconsciously give other people permission to do the same. As we are liberated from our own fear, our presence a u t o-matically liberates others.*[4]

---

[4] Williamson, M. (1992) A Return to Love: Reflections on the Principles of A Course in Miracles. Harper Collins.

Oprah Winfrey[5], media mogul and billionaire, experienced her own challenges pushing through the obstacles that others placed in front of her, while simultaneously having to muster the courage to fight for herself. As a young girl Winfrey was faced with many personal and family challenges that would ultimately shape her lens of the world. As she began to find her voice through writing and through media, Winfrey ultimately began a journey that would place her at a crossroads in her life where thinking small would be a crutch, and thinking big would be her divine intervention.

Winfrey was faced with a moment in time that would set her future up for unimaginable achievements. After working in news journalism for a number of years, and being told that she only could reach certain heights, she believed otherwise and continued to push forward, demonstrating her keen ability to connect with people from the deepest most authentic places that mattered the most.

---

[5] Oprah Winfrey is a media mogul, famous for her critically acclaimed Oprah Winfrey Show and Oprah Winfrey Network (OWN).

After accepting   an opportunity to host an early morning show in Chicago, Winfrey did something that was unheard of; she bet on herself. She decided to construct a deal that would ultimately set her up to be one of the few billionaires in America and the world. In her moment that mattered the most, Winfrey did not think small. And now, well, you know how Oprah Winfrey's life has played out, right? Playing small would have landed Winfrey in a position that was not meant for her. She chose to step into her purpose, and her gifts made more room for her than she ever could have imagined.

The question we must ask ourselves is, why do we play small? The answers are endless, but center on a few areas.   Limited beliefs and actions are motivated by fear, insecurities, low self-worth, and scarcity thinking.   Playing big means our actions are motivated by what brings us joy and fulfillment. That process is slower, more focused, and more deliberate.

When we think small, we are ultimately saying that we believe the outside world. We believe what others have told us, have programmed into our minds, that we are what *they* say we are. When we refuse to think big, to think about what's possible, we ultimately give the power of our lives over to people who have no knowledge about who we have been created to be.

But the flip side of that coin is that thinking big is not for the faint of heart. Thinking big is solely about one's ability to take ownership and accountability of what they have been inherently gifted to do in this world. When someone asks, "Why is that so difficult?" Well, the reality of that question is that it's not difficult to actually step into your greatness. But it is difficult for many of us to drown out the noise of the world and focus on what is real.

Playing small, thinking small, is not a byproduct of being small. It is, in fact, a byproduct of not understanding who you are, why you are, and what matters the most in this world. As a maturing professional, I recall vividly when colleagues or friends would suggest that I was thinking too big - that I was reaching for goals that I was not ready for. They would suggest to me that I take my time, and go through the normal process associated with typical professional growth.

And yes, there is something to be said about being patient and cultivating skills. But there's also something to be said about going for what you believe in and thinking so big that you push yourself to grow, to stretch, and to become what you are meant to become.

Did I listen? Sometimes. But ultimately my gut, my spirit, told me that I was meant for more. God had something in store for me that was so big, I had to throw away the worldly hesitation, the worldly fear, and lean into where I was being guided and stretched.

The fact is, when we think small, when we play small. We are saying to the universe that we simply don't believe in what has already been designed for us.

"Be leery of the price of conformity," said furniture salesman. All around us we see conformi see people who live in a space of "practical". But what really is being practical? Isn't practical just what we create because it is safe? "Practical" really is a worldly constructed idea. It is something that we actually have created to feel comfort and security. There is nothing "big" about conformity or practicality. They both make me cringe because they speak to an existence that is not designed by you or for you. They are created to keep you from your greatness.

April Beverly[6], author and copyright guru, shares that there are three signs that exist when one is playing small. The first is that NO crushes your spirit. When No crushes our spirit, we are in for a long, long journey. No is going to always be in existence. We are going to hear more No's than Yes's. Actually, we should welcome those No's. We should live for a No. Because a No says that we have room to grow and there is something greater on the other side. No doesn't mean No. No means go get better.

---

[6] Beverly, A. (2016) Shots Fired! How to write copy that pierces and opens wallets.BAAB Writing and Marketing Services.

In my lifetime I've heard more No's than I care to remember; but I am so happy I hear them. Each and every No forced me to be better, far more than any one Yes. And because of my No's, I was able to grow more, to stretch more, and become more thoughtful and focused about my craft.

My question for you is, "What do you do with your No's?" Do you stick them in the pile and disregard them, or do you treat them with the respect that they deserve? Do you tackle your No's with fierce conviction for your growth and empowerment? Respect and use your No's, because your Yes's don't tell you anything that you didn't already know.

The second sign of thinking small, Beverly asserts, is that we surround ourselves with insignificance. I mean, we have to stop and think about this one really deeply. What does it mean to surround ourselves with insignificance? Does this mean the people we call our friends don't add value and light to our lives? Does it mean the house and car, vacations and nice things we buy are simply distractions? Is it the way we camouflage ourselves to the world by creating personas that are not authentic? Thinking small pushes us to being something that we are not; because we are too damn scared to be what we truly are.

Surrounding ourselves with insignificant things, and even people who are insignificant to us, is just another way of running from what we have been created to be in this world. It is a manifestation of our deepest insecurities and greatest fears. *Insignificance is actually the most significant attribute of thinking small.*

The last barrier to thinking big, is when the going gets tough, we quit. Now this can be a touchy subject for so many people because no one likes to admit that they quit. But quitting is indeed a major element of thinking small. Quitting has been given a number of definitions by those of us who experience the quitting dynamic. But quitting is easy. It is the easiest action that we can take when thinking small. When we believe in ourselves, when we have confidence in what we can achieve, the option to quit never exists. Undoubtedly, when we think big, we can adapt, we can change directions, but we never will quit.

During her trials and struggles in her career, Oprah Winfrey never succumbed to the backlash of demeaning comments, the put downs about her appearance, nor the insults that she could not make it as a woman of color in a world led by white men. No, quitting was not on her agenda, no matter how hard she had it. No matter how much she had to endure, her ability to be resilient and focused on what she knew to be true about herself and her purpose in her life was her guiding light. When we think big, we have no time to think about quitting. Ask yourself, do I quit or do I adapt? There is a difference. Be honest with yourself. Because this is a game changer; when we are able to understand the clear delineation between quitting and adapting. *Those of us who think big, adapt. Those of us who think small, quit. End of story.*

We find ourselves in today's world so busy running away from the "No's," so busy quitting, so busy focused on what we can't accomplish or what we didn't accomplish -

that we find ourselves in a place of misery. N
don't have what we tried to attain, but becau
busy reacting to what the world proclaimed
what the world said that we should be doing; that we totally
lost focus of who we were built to be, the gifts that we have,
the purpose that we are meant for - we ultimately find ourselves resisting the exact thing that provides us the most
fulfilling and joyous life ever imagined.

We simply are spending our energy on the wrong
things. The degree of resistance you have is probably pro-
portionate to the amount of power waiting to be unleashed
once the "No" breaks through to a "Yes" and the call is followed[7]. Basically, once we shift the negative energy to positive energy, the universe opens up for us.

So, how do we do it? That's the big question. How
do we get out of the mindset of thinking small into living a
life of thinking big? How do we get courageous enough to

---

[7] Levoy, G. (2019) Why we play small: The role of resistance in following
our callings. Psychology Today. https://www.psychologytoday.com/us/
blog/passion/201903/why-we-play-small

_us on our plan-A? The plan that we were so passionately driven towards at one point in our lives. Or the plans that came to us later on in life, yet we found ourselves stuck in someone else's plan-A.

No, thinking big does not mean missing out on the details and the specifics of being focused on your goals. But thinking big means envisioning a life for yourself that you are equipped to achieve regardless of your self inflicted thoughts of inferiority. We begin by first acknowledging that we have a gift to the world; that we have a purpose to live in this world and provide the gift that we have within us. There is no other creature like you. You individually have been created to provide something to this world that is unique, that cannot be replicated, and it is within you to unlock it. Once you believe that you have this gift, the next step becomes easier.

Now we are ready to use No's; to live a life surrounded by significance and adapt, instead of quit. As April Beverly shares with us, these principles are essential in our ability to not only think big, but also achieve our greatest goals in life.

When we can use No's to unleash a deeper sense of learning and growth; when we can surround ourselves with significant components of life that have meaning and value, and we can adapt in the most challenging of times, we are on track to be big thinkers and even bigger doers.

Oprah Winfrey said it best, "Every decision I've ever made that led me to the right space and place in my life, I got there because I would listen to my inner voice." Your inner voice tells you every single day that you're not happy with what's going on in your life. That same voice tells you that you don't feel the way you want to feel. It tells you this, but it also tells you when you are the happiest - when you are thinking and doing the things that bring you joy in life, because those are the things that give you life.

What is it that gives you life? What is it that, when you think about it, is so abundant and so glorious and so huge, that is almost unimaginable. That's it. That freaking big. But I know you're scared, we all have been there. The question is, do you think it's worth staying there? And if you don't, then now is the time to set aside what you've been programmed to think, what you have been shamed into feeling, and begin to live the life that you were meant to live. It's time to think big and to stop playing small.

3. GOTTA HAVE A PLAN

Don't just BE

. . . .

So many of us in the world want all that life has to offer but we place limitations on what we are willing to do in order to get there.   Don't get me wrong, we all must have morals, values, and integrity.   But I'm speaking about those constraints that we create that have nothing to do with character and everything to do with pride: *I want to own a restaurant, but I'm not willing to go wash dishes to learn from the ground up...I want to be an author, but I don't want to commit to the time that it takes to sit down and actually write...I want to be a millionaire, but I have no clue about how I want to make my millions...I want to be known for something, but I've never sat down and actually written out what I am deeply passionate about.*

When we think about our plan-A, we can't just want to BE something. Our plan-A is requires more from us than just being. We can't just BE a dreamer, or BE excited about the possibility; we must do more than just BE. When we were younger our teachers and parents and friends always asked us "What do you want to BE when you grow up?" And most of us would have this great answer- a doctor or a lawyer, a professional athlete, an environmentalist or a teacher.

But all in all, we knew we wanted to be something,. We knew that being "something" meant something. Because we wanted to be something, we had goals in our lives as young children. "Being something" meant that you "were something".

As a child, being "something" was a far reach from actually understanding the journey of how to "become" something. There are not too many discussions, at an early age in life, on what the traits are of a person who is able to "become" the vision for their lives. The question *what do you want to be in life* is typically followed by very surface level discussion. What type of schools do you need to attend in order to become a doctor, or lawyer or teacher? What type of training do you need to become a musician or athlete?

But nowhere along the way did someone pull you to the side when you were a young child and say *there's more to just being something, you have to be more specific about how you become what you want to be in life.*

In Will Smith's depiction of Chris Gardner[8] in the movie *Pursuit of Happyness*, viewers were able to see a heart wrenching story of trauma, failure, and the resilience and fortitude of a man who didn't just want to BE, he want-

---

[8] Christopher Paul Gardner is a businessman and motivational speaker. During the early 1980s, Gardner struggled with homelessness while raising a toddler son. He became a stock broker and eventually founded his own brokerage firm Gardner Rich & Co in 1987.

ed to "BE-come something". Chris Gardner's story touched so many people around the world. As I watch this Black man fight to raise his son while being homeless, unemployed and hungry, I felt a sense of connection with him -not because I had the same lived experiences, but because the struggles and the challenges he faced made me reflect on my own experiences.

Chris Gardner was indeed a man that wanted to become more than just BE. In a popular interview shown on social media, Gardner speaks of five attributes of a person that seeks to do more than just BE - that we must have a plan, not just a goal.

He defines this plan as the C5 complex: BE clear, concise, consistent, compelling, and committed. But for the purpose of this book, I have taken a few liberties to adjust my personal C5 complex to BE clear, *curious*, consistent, committed, and *courageous*. And let's be clear, Gardner knows and SAYS, "Plan-B sucks!"

The first attribute Gardner speaks of in order to become, is that we must first be clear. Clarity is a gift that we seldom have when we have big vision. Being clear with oneself takes a lot of courage because we know that when we are clear about something, it forces us to have a laser focus on it. It demands our attention to a level that is typically unheard of in most endeavors. Being clear also means spelling out what we actually want to become and how we are going to achieve that goal. It means that we have to hold ourselves accountable to what we have not only thought of, but what we have determined to be the path to achieve our goals.

Typically, we fall into the space of quitting or stopping what we're doing because we think it just won't happen. We can always review if we were clear enough about what we do and how we want to accomplish our goals in life. Being clear allows us to ask ourselves the tough questions, to challenge ourselves, and ultimately to hold ourselves to the upmost accountability when we are diverting from the main goal.

The second attribute is being curious. Now, I did insert this attribute because I believe that being curious is essential to actually achieving big goals and ultimately achieving your plan-A.   Being curious is more about just having fly-by-night interests. When we are curious, we are setting the expectation for ourselves that we have a deep interest in something that is precious and important to us and that intrigues us to a place of extreme persistence.

The mystery of being curious is equally exciting. When we are not curious, we are essentially saying that we have no place to stretch ourselves. But when we lean in to a curiosity mindset, looking and seeking to find out the unknown, to examine the widely discussed, we ultimately land ourselves in a place of euphoric knowledge.

When we fail to be curious, we become slaves to what we have learned and what is in front of us.   Nothing else can enter our ethos, and we find ourselves doing the same things over and over again, achieving the same results - wondering why we're stuck in our plan-B.

The third attribute Gardner speaks about is consistency. The fact that we are not able to see things come to fruition in our lives has little to do with our capacity or talent level, and it has everything to do with our inability to be consistent. We must work at it. There's no magical remedy, or magical concoction, that provides us this mysterious answer to the question.

Consistency involves having a plan and sticking to it. Where we fail to be consistent is where doubt creeps in, where being abstract is probable. Consistency requires us to be committed with our behavior and habits. When I look back in my life and I think about the times I was inconsistent, I failed miserably. Those were the times when I didn't have a plan. I tried something for a few days or weeks, or maybe even a few months. But I didn't understand that time wasn't my obstacle. Building better habits, being consistent with those habits, and making sure that I saw growth in what I was doing, was the priority of the journey. *Consistency requires us to have our eye on the ball, not on the prize.*

The fourth attribute is commitment. Most of us don't have a commitment to our plan-A. That's why we settle for plan-B 's. It's not because we want plan-B's and it's not because we feel that the plan-B is better than plan-A. Remember, if plan-B was better than plan-A, then plan-B would be plan-A!

The question we must constantly ask ourselves is, "Are we really committed to our plan-A?" Are we committed to the things that we say we envision for our lives; that we want to grow within, that we want to excel in? In many cases we are committed to the dream, we are not committed to the journey. Once Gardner found his way in the stock market industry, he became committed. He understood that the journey was actually the prize. He understood that being committed meant doing things that he had never done, so that he could accomplish things that he had never dreamed of achieving. Commitment requires your full attention, determination, and sheer will.

The fifth attribute is courage. Again, this is one place where I deviated from Chris Gardener's 5C complex.

But, I chose courage because I firmly believe that without courage this entire journey of fulfilling your life's worth is void. We must have courage even in the place of fear. When fear takes control of us in ways that are unhealthy and detrimental to our lives, we realize the worst of our fears. But courage actually exists when fear creeps in and we still move forward and overcome - we find a way through. There is no shame in fear, but fear is meant to be used, not to be a user.

When I was sitting in that hospital waiting room, waiting to find out my diagnosis, I was very fearful. There were so many things on my mind - my family, things I had not accomplished in my life, the people with whom I had not mended relationships ; so many things that were sitting on my heart in fear, sitting right in my spirit.

But I had to come to grips with the reality that life would ultimately end one day; and if I was to live my life waiting on a signal of when it would end, that would make me the biggest fool to have ever lived. I had to make a decision to use my 5C complex, and to listen to my spirit, so that

I could live out my plan-A. I knew in my heart that my entire life, I had told myself that plan-B sucks; but I   acquiesced and lived someone else's plan-A.

It was time for me to become clear, curious, and consistent; to become radically committed and show a level of courage I had never demonstrated before. I knew that this meant that my life would totally change. I knew that things were going to happen I had no control over. But in that moment, when I decided to actually go after my plan-A, to be what God created me to be no matter the outcome - my spirit was in a state of peace that I'd never felt before.

So I started asking myself the questions about what I truly wanted to do with my life. What were the things that wanted to accomplish that fueled me, that motivated me, that made me contribute value to the world?

I dug deep into my soul and challenged myself to not give myself bullshit answers, to not gloss over what drove me, and to not be fixated on the superficial and sur-face level things that guide me to a place of regret and misery. I had to be honest with myself. I had to look myself in the mirror and and not let myself off the hook. I had to have a real conversation with myself: *Glenn, you are worthy of living a life that God created you to live and all you have to do is choose yes. You may not be thinking small, but you damn sure are acting like it.* That was the message I had to hear. But I acted like I was on everybody else's plan-A. I had succumbed to all of the covering behaviors- drugs, alcohol, sex, you name it. I covered myself up because I was not willing to unlock the gifts that God gave me. It was past time for me to accept my role in the reason why I was living out everybody else's plan-A.

The first step I took was to look at my purpose statement that I had written a couple of years earlier. I thought it lived within me since I had written it. But I actually had not unlocked it. Let me explain. After going through the process of writing down this passionate, meaningful purpose statement for my life, I presumed that it would move me to act. And so I went about the process of building my life around this purpose statement. But the one thing that I did not do, was hold myself fully accountable for the work that needed to happen in order for me to fully embrace living out what I had written down on paper.

I knew that my purpose statement was real. I knew that it spoke to all that I was created for in life. But what I had not done yet, was fully embrace the journey that was ahead of me. I had to stop drinking. I had to stop doing drugs. All of these abuses were distractions. It was that hurt and trauma and my lived experiences that guided me to this place.

The distractions were drowning out all those experiences and emotions that I felt, the same emotions that I needed to reveal my gifts for myself and the world. It's really funny actually. The things that I thought were helping me cover up all the hurt in my life, were the same things that were holding me back from living out God's purpose for my life.

This was my awakening moment. It was as clear as it could get right there in front of me. If I wanted to live the life that God created me to live, I would have to be accountable for what I decided to do next. The clarity that came over me was like a windstorm that hit me in the face. To quote a very popular slogan, "I needed to be the change that I wanted to see in the world."

4. FIND YOUR LANE

Gratitude, Gifts, and Grace

. . . .

You may have grown up in an era where you followed a certain set of rules and traditions. Or, you may be of a younger generation and have a nontraditional way of exploring life. Either way, if you are busy comparing and contrasting your life with everyone else's life, then you are going to be one miserable soul. And if you are going to have a ton of ideas and passions in life, you will see a few of those passions turn into something beautiful. But, I can assure you, if you focus on other people and not your passion, none of that will happen. You have to pick your lane, put your head down, and go play your game!

Building from purpose

From the beginning, building our firm Heart Work was not my initial goal. For so long, I had been searching for what my purpose was in life and really trying to understand what I would do with the gift I felt that I had to offer the world. Growing up, no one tells you that seeking your purpose in life may take up some meaningful time.

There is so much that goes into trying to understand what your purpose is in life and the journey is so uniquely different for each of us. As you begin to become more mature and experience life, what you want to do in your life may not become clear, but what you don't want to do definitely becomes clearer to you.

So much of what we do throughout our lives is trying to figure out where we fit in this world. And the truth is, most of us are just figuring things out, trying new things, and just having fun learning who we are. Undoubtedly, we kind of really were never lost, we were just experiencing this thing called life. So what does it really mean to find your lane? Why is it so important to us? The answer is rooted in so many levels of thought and perception. But I believe that the idea of finding our lane, on purpose, living in our plan-A, is a beautiful experience if we just allow it to unfold naturally.

When I was in college, I imagined that I would be either a government employee or teacher. But who knew? All I knew was that I was looking to learn more and experience more, more than I had ever experienced before. So I rarely said no to any opportunity. I was an open book. I taught elementary school as an after school teacher. I worked at a medical facility. I even coached tennis. I did whatever I could do to keep my mind and my spirit alive and healthy. I was super curious and I tried to really focus on the things that were meaningful to me.

But who has command of their plan-A in college? We know of the child prodigies and those kids who are just destined to do what they were undoubtedly created to do. We understand that they exist, but they are the exception not the rule. And so my plan-A really didn't exist in college. It didn't even exist post-college. But the journey to find our plan-A comes with obstacles that we never would've imagined that pose as plan-B. Those challenges sometimes make you presume that what you want out of life is not an actual reality. So you end up settling. As I began to see jobs that I enjoyed, but didn't feel a connection to, I began to understand that finding my lane was not just about the outcome, it was definitely about the journey.

So purpose was always a part of my consciousness. I was always thinking about why I am here and what I am supposed to be doing. Was I just going to get a job and go home, live for another 60 years and then die? That just didn't seem like my purpose. I didn't feel like there was less for me in the world. I felt like there was more for me in the world.

I believe that many of us know that there is more for us in this world. But the world can suggest otherwise through safe outlets that we trust unconditionally - either through family members, friends or the media, we can hear messages of simplicity and limited mindset. Don't get me wrong, simplicity doesn't mean less than. But the way we look at this type of messaging does matter. I believe we are all here to do extraordinary things in our own extraordinary way. So I was trying to figure out what that was for me. I was searching for more, and it was sitting right in front of me, waiting on me to notice it. Purpose is not something that we find. Purpose is something that is revealed.

Heart Work, the firm and my calling, is the manifestation of my journey of intentional and purposeful lived experiences. Heart Work came from my desire to find something that was always sitting right in front of me-my purpose. Because it was always there, it always showed up in everything I did, and other people saw it. And in their own way, they let me know they saw it, but it was up to me to understand what they were seeing. It was up to me to understand how my ideas were being manifested in those moments, for those reasons and purposes.

Over the years, while finding my space in the world, finding my voice, and going through the highs and lows of what life presented me, I was able to begin seeing clearly what I specifically wanted out of life. I share openly about living a life that really distracted me from what I truly wanted to do with my life, because context is extremely important in the intra-personal journey.

I believe that we accomplish anything when we acknowledge what we are willing to do. I had to be honest with myself about what I was willing to do in order to live a life of meaning and purpose. I may have been in the middle of figuring out my lane, but that didn't mean I couldn't begin to construct my life so that I could be prepared once my lane was clear.

In 2013 when I began to ask organizations to allow me to speak to their leaders about leading with love, I was met with a variety of responses. Most of them sounded something like, "Are you serious?" But I knew we were on to something that had drastically impacted me in ways that I never would have imagined. All those years of leading with force and not being compassionate, led me to a place of extreme resolve. And when I saw what compassion, love and empathy did in the workplace, I was forever trans-formed.

This feeling was heavy; this transformation that was going on in my heart and my spirit was more than just an aha moment. In those moments, my eyes began to under-stand how purpose is revealed. The lane that I had been searching for, for so long, was being revealed to me.

So I just began to do the work. I offered my services as a "non-fee". I emailed people, I popped up on people's jobs, and called all the friends that I had to let them know I was leading with love. And yes, it started off super slow. People would act as if they understood the premise of lead-ing with love, but they couldn't get their minds around how it would land with their teams.

But I persisted and kept asking. By this point, being a few years in, I had just enough in my spirit to hold me upright and to keep moving forward. It would have been easy to just allow this feeling in my gut to wither away and focus on my day job. But I knew better (because I had been down this road before); when your purpose reveals itself to you, it's as if you are blind to the naysayers. You have a super-power that says you can knock down the walls and clear the fields of any obstacles. And you can do it, just keep going.

The lane that is created for us is the lane for us. And when this happens, when we find the lane that we exist in, plan-A must be plan-A. In that moment, we can honestly say to ourselves that plan-B sucks! So I kept pushing forward, and I refused to let go of what would eventually become the Heart Work Leadership Group.

After writing my first book, *Heart Work*, I teamed up with my friend and now business partner to continue the work of leading with love. Ultimately, the idea came to me that renaming our firm from Leadership Matters to Heart

Work would be just the statement that I wanted to make. All the time that I had spent sharing the message of leading with love with leaders who heard me, and many that didn't, would now be clear to them in our name.

Heart Work symbolizes all of what my purpose in life is; it represents everything that I feel and believe in about the world and the living, breathing beings in it. Heart Work is my plan-A, not because it's what I always wanted to do since I was a child, but because it's what has been inside of me as far back as I can remember. When you figure out what your plan-A is, it most likely will not be a surprise.

What hinders us?

There are so many things that we see as obstacles in our lives. And when we hear other people's stories, it's really easy to deflect and just say that their story isn't my story so I can't relate. But not relating to someone else's story isn't the fundamental issue. The issue is that we have been used to obstacles in our lives that we simply don't know how to address.

This was the case for me. It wasn't about relating to other people's stories; it wasn't about finding my story in somebody else's experience. It was really about having the tools that I needed in order to move forward with what I believed was meant for me. These are the questions that we ask ourselves when we try to find purpose in our lives, when we all have these types of challenging question and few answers.

Challenges in choosing your lane - Gratitude

- Where do I begin?
- How can I be sure?
- What happens if I fail?

When we are up against these challenges, I found for myself, and for every single person in the world, is that we must know that gratitude is life. We must start every day with a grateful heart and live and end each day with the spirit of gratitude. That's how we begin to fight the obstacles and challenges that will arise in our lives as we walk through our personal journey in purpose.

So how do we use gratitude to help us live better lives? Where do I begin? This is the age old question when we are seeking out something that's greater than what we have control over. Indeed the answer is in the question itself - *Where do I begin?* Begin. There it is. The answer to the most mind-boggling and complex question of every purpose seeker - We must begin. And when gratitude exists in your life every single day, and in every single aspect of it, beginning becomes easier, and easier, and easier.

After we figure out where we begin, we turn to the question, "How can I be sure?" And that's a question that will stop you in your tracks, and literally derail all the work you've done up to that point. Once again, we can find the answer to this question in the question. *We cannot be sure.* Being sure is not something that's going to happen in the process of revealing purpose in your life.

Shortly after we figure out that we just have to begin, and that we can never really be sure, we ultimately must task ourselves with the high bar of asking the question "What happens if I fail?" Oh wait, that's such an oxymoronic question to ask ourselves. What happens if I fail? Well, nothing happens. Nothing happens if we fail, because if we are asking this question, we have already stopped our progress to begin with. The idea that a life well-lived is a life without failure, is a misunderstanding of what life is really about. A better question to ask is "When I fail, what will I learn?"

Choosing your lane - Use your gifts

* Get out of your head
* Release your gifts
* Try something; anything

Our gifts are critical in how we use the power to choose our own lane. We shouldn't be concerned with how we are seen, better yet, we should be focused on what we envision. The popular scripture reads "your gifts will make room for you". But our gifts only can make room if we can *get out of our own head*. So many of us have the tendency to over think, over process, and under deliver on the promise of our gifts. We find solace in the fact that we have a passion or idea, but stay in a space of safety and dare not jump out on the ledge called life.

If we want to choose our own lane in life (our plan-A), then getting out of our head and into the world is the first step to *releasing our gifts*. Each of us has gifts that we have either known about since we were young, or over time we just realized that we were gifted in doing a special thing. In most cases we use our gifts every single day of our lives. Hopefully, we have been able to see our gifts in the things that we are passionate about, the people we have met, and the experiences that we have had.

Intentionally using our gifts so that we can be open to choosing the lane that we were specifically meant for is a conscious, deliberate behavior. When we pause and find ourselves asking how do we use our gifts, the simplest answer is to just get out of our own way and use them the best way we know how.

I pushed myself to use my gifts. I tried anything and everything. Mind you, healthy choices are the best choices. But trying new things, experiencing new places, and opening yourself to the unknown is one of the best ways we can truly see our gifts represented in the world.

When should we take a detour? - Use grace

- When inspiration, not fear, is moving you

- Ask yourself, "Am I starting, stopping, or both?"

- Ask yourself "What am I moving towards?" and "What am I leaving?"

Finding our own lane is not only about figuring out what our purpose is in life. Finding our own lane is also about the experience of life, the joys of life, and the suffrage of life. In this search of our personal purpose, we often find ourselves in spaces that lead us to make hard choices. Do I go for it no matter what? When do I abandon what I thought was my purpose in life to do something totally different? These are important questions, and yet if our mindset is focused on an outcome, and not the journey, we ultimately will miss the most beautiful aspect of the process itself.

If and when we ever figure out our plan-A in life, the one aspect that we must take into consideration is harnessing a spirit of grace. And not solely the grace that we extend to others, but grace that it takes to forgive ourselves for the failures and missed opportunities that will inevitably happen along our journey of life.

You may ask why is grace so important. And my silly response would be, if you know you know! But on a serious note, grace supports our spirit of resilience and perseverance. Grace is required, because we don't know what life will bring; we don't understand fully the ebbs and flows of all that we will experience as we live a life of purpose.

But we do know that there will be detours, obstacles, and challenges that will be presented. Grace allows us to be present in all of those moments and yet continue forward. Grace is precious, filling, and empowering. It's all those things that bring you peace, security, and the will to continue

But when do we know when and how to take a detour in our journey while giving ourselves grace in the same moments? The realization that I found myself in was that I needed to define my "why" before I could make detours that may be misguided by fear or insecurities. When inspiration, not fear, is moving us to do something new or different, we must pay attention. Does this mean that we do something or change something? Not necessarily. But it allows us the time and space to ask more questions. Am I starting or stopping something, or am I doing both? What am I moving towards and what am I abandoning?

When we are able to acknowledge healthy obstacles that exist to challenge our thinking, or pressure us to go deeper, it is incumbent for us to pause and think. This is when grace is necessary. Why? Because when our journey is interrupted, or derailed, we can find ourselves in a space of blame and shame. But grace is all we need in order to understand that detours can be the healthiest, most rewarding experience of our journey. The answers are not often going to come easily in our search for our lane; the questions are plentiful. But sharpening our iron happens in a variety of ways because plan-A will always bring more challenges than plan-B.

Again, giving yourself grace is the key to this step in the process of finding your lane. I can't, nor can any other person, give you the answers to your questions. But the tools (or the questions you should ask) are essential in not getting stuck when the ebbs and flows do happen. There's more on grace later in the book.

5. YOU'RE NOT ALONE

"Alone" is where the work happens

. . . .

We may feel lonely on this journey, but we are never alone.

Emotions serve a purpose and loneliness is an emotion. Loneliness alerts us to something happening, or not happening. This emotion, like all emotions, can be a place of self discovery or self destruction. If being alone is stirring up emotions of loneliness, a great question to ask yourself is, " What am I missing in this moment?" and "How can I grow in this moment?"

Alone may just be lonely, or not

In my youthful imagination, I was always some type of politician. When I found myself running for public office in the city of Atlanta, it was a whirlwind of an experience. Initially, people were excited, eager, and willing to help support me in my endeavor. But shortly into the process of running for mayor, though there were people around me, I felt a sense of being alone. This idea of being alone is tricky. Because being alone and being lonely are technically different, but can become the same (if we allow it).

I was not alone, but I was lonely. Who could I have turned to in those moments of aloneness? I had not personally known of anyone that had run for public office, and the fact of the matter was, I was doing something that most of my supporters could not logically see themselves doing.

Was I out there by myself running for office? Well, it depends on how you look at it. Yes, I was the person that was running for the office. Yes, I was the person that was putting my name on the line to win that race. But I wasn't by myself, and though I felt alone, I was not alone. If you have had the awesome honor of doing something big, bold, and audacious, then you may have experienced the state of being alone. And even more so, you probably have felt the emotion of loneliness .

What does this really mean? What does it mean when we interchange the words alone and lonely? What does it mean when we find ourselves in a state of being alone, and feeling lonely? It simply means that we're human. I found that when I was running for office, when I was in the trenches every single day making phone calls, knocking on doors, and asking for contributions, I wasn't alone. People were out there working on my behalf, I just didn't or couldn't always see them.

But the moments I was physically by myself and even some moments when there were others around, I could feel extremely lonely. Not because I was being self-centered or not being present, but because I had thoughts and feelings within myself that I just believed no one else could understand. Have you experienced that before? That feeling of not seeing where or who you can turn to when you are in the midst of the journey.

What came to me later in that experience was that those feelings were feelings that I didn't know were OK to have. Those feelings were not only OK to have, but they were natural to have. I began to understand that loneliness is not a bad thing; that loneliness is an emotion that is natural, normal and even healthy.

I learned from that experience that being "alone" is where the work actually happens. I know it may sound confusing, right? The idea of being alone, feeling lonely, and being able to accomplish something audacious at the same time may seem counter-intuitive.

But being alone can actually allow you to be laser focused on what you're trying to achieve. What I found was that in those moments when I was alone, I was dialed in more than ever before. I began learning that the state of being alone and the emotion of feeling lonely could co-exist in a transformative way right before your eyes.

Yes, it may seem confusing a little bit to talk about being alone and loneliness. Who tells us that we are actually alone? Is it our inner voice or are we listening to the voices around us?

As my campaign for public office evolved and grew into a small team of supporters, I participated in more television and radio interviews, and a host of public appearances; I experienced those enriching feelings of what can happen in a state of being "alone" or feeling lonely. There was meaning in those spaces; emotions that I had not ever imagined I would reflect on. I was experiencing that "cool emptiness," or state of presence that author Pema Chodron[9] addresses in *Welcoming the Unwelcome*.

When we are in our lane of purpose and giving our all to our plan-A, being "alone" and feeling lonely, are more common than we sometimes want to admit. But the reality of both are not only natural, but they are normal and some may say, required.

---

[9] Chodron, P. (2019) Welcoming the Unwelcome. Shambhala.

How to use your "alone" mindset

- Aloneness can derail you, or ignite you

- Get comfortable being uncomfortable

- Appreciate what is right in front of you

When we get to a place in life where we are not feeling as though we have someone to turn to, we have to consider how we are using our "alone" mindset. We should first recognize that being alone and feeling lonely are not the same, and aloneness can derail you or ignite you. A question you can ask yourself is, "What am I doing when I am alone or feeling lonely?" If I am alone, by myself, what is happening in that moment? Am I actually learning something more? Am I feeling something more when I experience that aloneness?

If we are able to get comfortable with being uncomfortable, just maybe we are able to gain perspective into why we are where we are. Is it just by coincidence or is it intentional that we arrive in a place where we have time to be with ourselves, to think for ourselves?

This state of aloneness gives us an opportunity to be introspective, by which we can actually process some of the most important and valuable lessons and blessings in our lives. This is how purpose is revealed. This is how finding one's lane is manifested. Transformation does not happen in comfortable places and spaces. I know it seems like more than a few questions to ask, but introspection is the path to self-awareness.

How often do we take notice of what is standing right in front of us? Aloneness is not an unhealthy space unless we allow it to be. What have you been missing in your journey to plan-A? What has been staring you directly in your face, whispering in your ear, rumbling in your spirit? Whatever it is, whatever it may be, being in aloneness and feeling lonely can be the opportunity that you have been searching for. Try to begin getting comfortable with your opportunity of aloneness, and using it to gather your deepest thoughts, hear your inner voice, and develop your superpower - your purpose.

Make "aloneness" transformative

- Recharge your personal wellness
- Realize more productivity
- Do things you enjoy

This may or may not come as a complete surprise, but aloneness is transformative. It allows us to recharge our personal wellness through means by which we normally would not activate for ourselves. The intensity of how we allow alone time to become a value for us is enriched by our ability to understand clearly what aloneness really means. We simply are never alone, whether we are by ourselves in the physical or not.

Think about the things that you do when you are alone. Maybe it's exercising, reading, or meditating. Maybe alone time for you is an opportunity to just be at peace, to not think about anything, but just be in that moment. Where can you experience this type of personal wellness, other than aloneness?

You may say that being alone is more than being well, and when you're alone you don't feel as though you can lean on anyone or gather any wisdom from anyone. Personally, I believe that we must have moments where there is no one to turn to other than ourselves, in order to fully reveal what is resting within our spirit.

When you require something that is greater than physical interaction, it's time to look within yourself to figure out what you actually need. If you ever have had one of these moments, then you can understand how aloneness can reset your frame of heart, mind, and wellness.

When we experience aloneness, we are able to realize greater productivity. Yes, obviously teamwork does make the dream work, and we can get a lot of things done together as team. But when I talk about more productivity, I'm speaking about the ability of the intra-personal transformation that happens when we are within our own space.

I remember in the middle of the campaign when I had lost so much weight and I was visibly tired and frustrated to the point of wanting to quit. I began to spend time just within my mind and heart, even when there were people around. Some people refer to this as heart intelligence. I would take moments of time to just breathe and allow my mind, emotions and heart to connect and arrive at centeredness.

At the time I didn't really know if it was working or if it meant anything. But ultimately, what I found was that those moments shaped what would be some of the most transformative learning experiences I have ever had. What are you doing in your aloneness to benefit your awakening? What are you intentionally doing in your space and time with yourself, when you feel that you are lonely?

The amazing thing about aloneness is that you can make it really fun too, because we must do things we enjoy even when we are alone. It's as simple as watching a movie that you know no one else likes, or watching that silly television show. But it is also a walk in the park, an ice cream adventure, or simply sitting still. No matter what it is that you do, do whatever it is that you enjoy while you are alone. It doesn't matter what you do when you're feeling lonely, but what really matters is that you do something that allows you to see the meaning in that experience, because every single moment we have has value. Aloneness is not an empty experience, unless we choose for it to be. So, choose wisely.

6. LASER FOCUSED

Keep your wits about you

. . . .

You want to achieve your dreams? Then start focusing on making your dream a reality. Sounds simple enough, but far too many of us have had dreams deferred. I recall the first time I read the poem *Harlem / A Dream Deferred*. It stopped me in my tracks. I wondered what it meant; what was Langston Hughes[10] trying to say?

----

[10] James Mercer Langston Hughes was a poet, social activist, novelist, playwright, and columnist from Joplin, Missouri. (1951) Harlem / A Dream Deferred

What happens to a dream deferred? / Does it dry up

Like a raisin in the sun? / Or fester like a sore--

And then run? / Does it stink like rotten meat?

Or crust and sugar over--like a syrupy sweet?

Maybe it just sags / like a heavy load.

Or does it explode?

Between a rock and a HARD place

Aren't our plan-B's just another dream deferred? Years ago, when I was speaking to audiences for no-cost fees, I would consistently be asked if my presentations were written down somewhere. I took the questions as compliments, but I summed them up to people just wanting to follow-up on what I had shared. And I always noticed that so many people would ask me to share more details about my stories. It made me begin to think that I needed to be more intentional about what I shared and how I made it relevant for those who were listening.

In that moment, I became more aware of my responsibility as a speaker, a teacher, and someone who was inspiring others through my experiences. So I began to think about what it meant to be an author. I wanted to speak, but I also wanted to write. Now, keep in mind, that this was in the beginning stages of my leadership practitioner career. I was still figuring out what I enjoyed, what I disliked, and what pushed me to be better. But I knew deep inside if I wanted to have more impact, I would have to hone my skills, and become a student of my craft.

About halfway into my career of public speaking and leadership development, I began to get clearer on what I specifically wanted to do with my work. This realization came about from the practice of writing. I have been writing since the days of my retail career, where this all started by the way. And because of that, I have accumulated so many articles and notes and papers that were all about my personal beliefs and professional insights on leadership love, family, and all the things that I personally feel are important for any leader to know.

It was so crazy, for all of my life, people have been telling me to focus on one thing or another.   And for the first time in my life, in those moments of clarification, publicly speaking and writing about my journey to purpose was my life. I had always enjoyed sharing, seeing people being inspired to do more for themselves, so that they can do more for others.

Public speaking was something I knew in my soul I was created to do. But writing was an experience that literally surprised the hell out of me. For four years I had been writing and didn't even realize   the book that I wanted to write, was right there in front of me. Now it was up to me to write the story that I had been writing for so long.

But unbeknownst to me, I didn't know how long this process would take. From that moment, to the moment of publication, it would literally take four years to publish my first book. If you had told me in that moment how long it would take, I'm not sure that I would have been encouraged to write my first book.

So we must ask ourselves how focused are we on our purpose? How committed are we to doing the work? These questions must be answered with the truth. If we're not ready to be focused on what is a priority in our lives, then we surely will be swayed towards plan-B. In those times I was struggling between my plan-A and my plan-B, I fought like hell to find my focus. But as we know, just because our vision becomes clearer, doesn't mean our journey becomes easier.

I would often turn to people looking for guidance, but as I always say, it's you who must make the decision and choose when and how to move forward. I had to come up with ways to stay focused amid all of the madness that was happening around me.

So there are a few things we must remember when we're trying to focus on our priorities, and create a life for ourselves that was not created by someone else. When we are focused on our plan-A, we must remember these things:

What we need to remember:

- Today is the only promise - *yesterday has passed and to-morrow has yet to come, so what you do with today is the only thing promised to you. Do today what you can.*

- Comparisons are make-believe - *imposter syndrome and comparison mania will stop you in your tracks and throw you off of your game.*

- Intention is undefeated - *when you put your mind to something with intention, only YOU can stop you from achieving your most ambitious goals.*

Today is the only promise

Unfortunately, there comes a time in one's life when you begin to look around and see people in your circle leaving the earthly world. Because of age, at some point we begin to realize that we are losing friends, family and love ones. The old adage is that the only thing that is certain in life is death and taxes. Well, I'm not so sure about taxes anymore, but death, I'm 100% certain.

By my mid 30s, I had already seen lives lost too soon, whether through acts of violence or just natural reasons. I was becoming well aware of the reality of life and death. I was scared and mostly confused, but recognized that I was seeing clearly what the the cycle of life really looked like.

I had to realize that "today" is the only day that was promised for me. And I know we hear it and see it so much, and we often say it ourselves, that *tomorrow is not promised*. But it is not promised. It is truly the most factual statement you can ever make. Tomorrow is not promised. Today is the only promise. We must do what we can with the moments that we have right before us; there is no guarantee of the next moment, so if we actually take pride and joy in what we are experiencing, then we can live in the moment that we are in - being present in what is real. That is living. That is focusing on our plan-A.

Comparisons are make-believe

If you want to get into a deep conversation with somebody, especially in the year 2021, bring up the topic of comparison mania. Ten years ago, I could not have told you about anything related to comparison mania because I could not define what comparison mania was. But, coupled with imposter syndrome, comparison mania has so many of us not believing in ourselves because we're so focused on other people. It is indeed the oxymoron of the century.

Growing up, I never had an issue with confidence. My mother's influence in my life as a young child constantly pushed me to do better and instilled in me the idea that I could do anything in the world that I wanted to; and that all things were possible. Now, was she stretching it to say that you can do "anything" in life? Kind of. But, ALL things ARE possible. That's how I grew up. But even with that level of confidence as a young person and maturing into an adult, I still fell victim to imposter syndrome. So we can only imagine those of us who don't grow up around that type of confidence culture and fall into this idea that we are not good enough.

I had fallen squarely into that dark hole myself. But, in my moment of purpose and figuring out my plan-A, I found myself questioning if I could actually stand toe to toe with my counterparts. The problem with that frame of thinking, was   that was the wrong mindset. I was allowing my comparison mania to take me into imposter syndrome.

What is it about this imposter syndrome that plagues so many of us? Why is it that when we actually figure out what our purpose is in life, we begin to question ourselves? Where does this mindset come from? Is that nature versus nurture? Or is it nature and nurture? I believe it is the combination of the two.

It is this idea that we must be better than the next person, or we must first validate our expertise to the world, in order to justify our place in the world. But what I had to figure out on my own, through lots of prayer and deep reflection, is that *God created every living thing in this world on purpose, with purpose, and for purpose.*

And you don't have to believe in God to acknowledge that every living thing in this world is here on purpose. It is the cycle of life that we all are a part of. And so, if you can agree with me, that each of us is here on purpose, with purpose, and for purpose, then you should also be able to agree that there is no such thing as imposter syndrome; because you are who and where you are supposed to be.

That is how we are able to stay laser focused in a world that seeks to pull us into comparison mania. There is no comparison. You are the answer. We are the answer. Together, we form the answer.

Intention is undefeated

This word "intention" has received quite the attention because the legendary Oprah Winfrey speaks about it so often (and because I am an obvious Oprah fan). I love the word "intention" as much as she does. But early on in my career, I never used the word or even thought of the word as being so critical to my personal and professional success.

The word "intention" speaks volumes for those of us who are seeking to stay laser focused on our plan-A. And the reason is because intention speaks to our level of accountability, our commitment to purposefully achieving the goals that we have set for ourselves. I love the word "intention", because intention is undefeated.

When I was beginning to think about what this business of *leadership practitioner* would look like for me, I didn't know what to make of it. Was I going to be speaking to people? Was I going to only be facilitating leadership sessions? Or was it something of a combination of sorts? In the midst of trying to figure things out, I was getting lost in questions, when I actually had the answer right in front of me.

I needed to remember that the shortest distance between two points is a straight line. I wanted to inspire people to live better, so that they could lead better. That was my intention. So, if that was my intention, then all I had to do - was do just that. Once I understood that, I stopped over thinking what "this" would look like as a business, and started acting on what my intention was; and then the business began to take shape.

Does that make sense? Do you understand how this happens? We must first understand our intention, to ultimately begin to move towards our plan-A. And when we are able to just move forward based on our intention, everything will take shape in the right course. We just don't have to have the answers to the test in the beginning of the class. Our focus should be to speak our intention and move forward. Yes, there are some ins and outs that we must construct for our sanity, our health, and our ability to stay centered. But ultimately, the job is very simple. So, ask yourself, "What is my intention?" And then lay out a simple format and go to work.

There are a number of reasons why it took me four years to write my first book. Some were reasonable and some were not. Many of those obstacles that I encountered, were created because I was trying to figure out all the answers; I was trying to construct all the right decisions and manners in which I would move forward into writing my first book.

Though I had an intention, I was lost in trying to design every specific component of something that I had no prior knowledge of creating. Have you been there? That place when you are doing something that you have never done before, while simultaneously attempting to get it perfect. Really? Does that have any element of logic? No, it doesn't. When we are on a journey that we have never been on, we must recognize that we will not have the answers; we cannot write a perfect script; we will never get it done if we are always trying to get it perfect.

The tide changed in my book writing process when I decided to "just do it". I was determined to write my first book. I gave myself a deadline, constructed the outline, and went to work. As I began to write, on schedule, every single day, writing towards my outline, I found that even on my tough writing days, the writing got done. We must know that every day that we are in living within our intention, that things won't go well all the time.

But if we are consistent, and intentional, we will be able to move forward and see progress. And with progress

we begin to understand more and more that we are not im-
posters in our bodies. We begin to see ourselves as who we
truly are; we are meant for this world - on purpose. And imposter syndrome becomes the *purpose syndrome*. We feel
like comparing ourselves less to others because we begin to
see ourselves as who we are meant to be. Intention and
consistency cancel out imposter syndrome and comparison
mania.

When we hear people say, "I didn't achieve my goal
because someone else stepped in the way and stopped me,"
we must understand that no one can stop us from achieving
anything we put our minds to; because all things are possible. Only you can stop you from achieving the goals you
have in your life; only YOU can stop YOU from achieving
your plan-A.

Our mindsets must be designed in a way that we
understand that all things in life are not probable, but all
things in life are possible. And with that, we must design
our minds to understand that intention is undefeated because we are meant for this world, we are meant for a pur-

pose, and because of that there is no failing in the process of intention.

How to begin

- Write what you want - *be specific on your goals.*
- Follow your routine - *develop and focus on your routine.*
- Done is better than perfect - *get it done, first; then get it right.*

Write what you want

Now let's talk specifics, because we must get really specific about "how we begin" the process of being laser focused on our goals. All too often I hear people talk about taking mental notes and thinking about what to do next.

Don't get me wrong, that sounds really good and feels good, and makes a good topic in conversation. But, if you are not writing it down, it doesn't exist. Look, let's keep this really simple. Think it, write it, and then do it.

Now, it doesn't get any simpler than that. We must stop making this process of achieving our goals in our life so complex. If you have stopped feeling like you're an imposter, and you have stopped comparing yourself to everyone else, then all you need to do is keep it simple and make it plain.

I had been writing my first book for years, and I didn't even know it. But once I figured out that I had a foundation from which to write , my anxiety went down. Whatever you're doing in your life, and you find yourself over analyzing it - first, ask yourself one question: What exists right now that I can pull from that can be my starting point to move forward? Whatever it is that you're looking to do, you have a starting point. You may not think it's a starting point. You may not think it's meaningful, but you must trust that what you have is enough to start with.

The mistake that we make so often is that we are searching for things outside of our natural environment. What does that mean? It means that we have assets and resources available to us that we never think of. We have created things over the course of time that we never pull from. Because we don't reflect on "what we have," we are constantly reflecting on "what we need". *Need* is a formidable opponent in the journey for "getting things done".

Remember, for so many years I was trying to design this book idea that would be perfect for people to read and that would speak eloquently about all the things that I experienced in my life. And it would be able to capture readers hearts and minds. But because I was trying to capture what I needed to write this amazing book, I negated the fact that I could just draw from what I already had created. I have been writing for years. I had been taking notes, jotting down my thoughts, and reflecting on all these experiences that I had in life that were meaningful to me; and I knew would be meaningful to others. I spent years doing that. My question to you is, how many years have you been spending on seeking what you need, as opposed to using what you have?

Right now, it's time to get out of your head and get it down on paper. A bold plan-A can't wait for perfect. You have all you need. Write it down. Plain and simple. The process seldom makes sense in the beginning. But that's the whole point. We must start before we can get anywhere even close to the finish line.

Follow your routine

If you don't have a routine, that's your routine. I know how we can get so disheveled and frustrated because of life and all that happens outside of our careers. But having a routine it's critically important to achieving any type of goal, especially our most ambitious goals. As I began to get more focused on writing my first book, I realized that there were certain conditions I could not write in and there were certain things that I needed to effectively achieve my daily writing goals.

Historically, I had never had a problem with creating routines about things that I felt were important to me, but this was different. When we are focused on something that is so audacious, and big and bold, we can fall into the idea that we have it under control. Without developing parameters and routines that guide us to the finish line, we will get derailed. I had to recognize that plan-A's are not achieved without a routine. Question: What is your routine for your most audacious goals?

If you can spell out specifically what you do, how you do it, why you do it, and when you do it, then you are on a great path. But if you can't, then we must pause right here and begin to construct the framework for routines that will enable you to actually get to the finish line.

There's not only one answer for every person when creating routines, this process must be unique to your personality, your environment, and a host of other variables that exist in your life. But, aside from those unique variables in your life, there are some steps we can take to actually begin to develop a really effective routine to achieve our goals.

By this point you have written your goal. Your intention is clear and specific. Now we just need to develop a routine and focus on being consistent in our routine. We first must ask ourselves how much time am I going to spend daily, weekly, and monthly on my goal? Second, we must map out a schedule with a time commitment.   Note, we must remember that it doesn't do us any good to create an unrealistic routine/schedule. And also, we must understand that things will come up and we will have to adapt within our routine.

That being said, the last piece of this puzzle is to create an accountability resource and select an accountability partner.   Make sure that whomever you select, they are not your "rubber stamp" fan club. We need honest, clear, and inspiring accountability partners to support us in our journey.

The only hard and fast rule here is be honest with yourself and do not include anyone in this process that is going to stroke your ego and not hold you to the standard that you expect from yourself. If we are going to be serious about accomplishing our goals, living in our plan-A, then we must be equally as serious as developing a routine and holding ourselves accountable to what we want to create. Remember, only YOU can stop YOU.

Done is better than perfect

When we are trying to get everything so perfect, such that we are spending countless hours, days, weeks, and months on something, we will never get it done. I hate to tell you, but done is better than perfect. Get it done, first - then get it right.

Again, this goes back to the old imposter syndrome and comparison mania. Why are you so busy trying to get something perfect when you haven't even gotten it done? It's not because you are a perfectionist, it's not because you just need to have it right before anybody reads it. It's only because you are concerned about stuff you have no control over. Yes! It's time to get out of your own head and get it down on paper and get moving. Control what YOU can control. It's time that you release the IF's, AND's and BUT's mindset, and focus on DONE.

There are a whole lot of "could be" Pulitzer Prize winners out there in the world who have never written a single word. There are quite a few basketball stars who've never seen an NBA arena. There are a myriad of doctors and lawyers and teachers who have never once stood up in their profession and illuminated their gift; because they just were trying to get it perfect - and ended up never getting it at all. Done is better than perfect folks. Get it done first and then worry about the next steps.

How many times in your life have you been working on a project or something related to your personal life that was important to you? You thought about it over and over again, processed it, thought about it again, slept on it, and just let it linger in your mind forever. How did it turn out? Maybe it turned out well for you, maybe it didn't. Or maybe it just turned out how it was going to turn out. What am I getting at here?

I am merely suggesting that though being thoughtful is a valuable attribute, overthinking every single thing in your life is not going to get you learning and achieving. The mindset of getting things done first is not about negating the presence of thoughtfulness. It is about being mindful that, if we allow ourselves to, we can overthink just about anything.

For 3 1/2 years I thought deeply and "intellectually" about this grand book that I was going to write. And so I'm sure that some goodness came out of that time period. I am also pretty certain that the book ended up how the book ultimately was going to end up - written! Yes, the book ultimately was written. That was my intention - to write a book about my lived experiences, and that's exactly what happened. After thinking about it and processing it for a fairly long time, the book ultimately was written. Could I have written it in less than four years? I am sure of it. What did I take away from that process? Being thoughtful and taking action are not mutually exclusive (unless you choose for them to be).

So what's the moral of this principle? Well, if you need me to say it one more time for the people in the back of the room; get er' done!

How to persist

- Set micro wins - *achievements, no matter how*
  your fire. Take the time to set goals that you c... ...
  ately achieve, and then celebrate them.

- Eliminate distractions - *in many cases we define our dis-*
  tractions as therapy or fun; and that may be the case in
  some instances, but if your "distractions" are prohibiting
  you from dedicating time to your priorities, then it's time
  that you either decrease them or eliminate them all to-
  gether. No one can tell us how to manage our time, but if
  we want to be focused on the goal at hand, then we must
  make the right decisions about the wrong things.

- Prioritize self-care - *Taking care of yourself is a require-*
  ment for taking care of business. When we are so focused
  on what we want out of life, it is easy to forget that we are
  human and still need to care for ourselves.

Set micro wins

So I know the whole "get 'er done" mindset can be a little bit off putting. But, we can build strategies around the "get 'er done" mindset. The first principle involves setting micro wins for ourselves. One of the best ways to persist, is to see yourself winning. How do we do that? How do we set our-selves up for micro wins while trying to not get blinded by the macro goal?

Let's start by acknowledging that we are not going to achieve macro goals by solely focusing on the macro goal. Setting micro wins begins with reverse engineering our process, then developing milestones that allow us to see our growth and success.

Remember, at this point, we have created a routine to accomplish our goals. And because of that, we can set milestones that we can reach in very quick order; that will allow us to see progress and give us more confidence to move forward. The tangible value of setting micro wins is obvious; but there are psychological benefits to setting micro wins as well.

We know that everyone will not be a supporter of what we're doing or even understand what we're trying to accomplish. But when we set micro wins, hitting those milestones consistently, we mentally become stronger. We are then able to drown out anything that is antithetical to our mission of achieving our primary goal.

As we set micro wins, we also contribute to our overall development. We are able to see in real time the effect of setting, accomplishing, and learning from our goals. We are able to evaluate ourselves in real time and make adjustments and re-construct certain aspects of our plan-A. All of these steps are within the process that we are experiencing and they contribute to us living within our purpose.

There is simply no losing when we set micro wins for ourselves. But when we don't set micro wins, and we are only focused on the result, we can lose dramatically. Because there is growth in the process, there is confidence building in the process. And while we are setting micro wins, we must know that we will have micro failures; failure is a requirement in any journey that is worth investing in. *Micro wins without micro failures is a macro disaster.*

Eliminate distractions

How we focus on our plan-A, squarely aligns with how we eliminate distractions in our environment. Most of the time, we define distractions by tangible things such as technology or outings with friends. But distractions can take on a variety of definitions. Distractions are anything that take up space within our thoughts and habits. And though we know that there are some really healthy distractions, there are those distractions that don't support us in a healthy way. These unhealthy distractions compromise what we are trying to accomplish in our lives.

We must be strong enough, focused enough and committed enough to *make the right decisions about the wrong things*. I've made more bad decisions than I care to remember. And thankfully those bad decisions have not resulted in dire consequences. So I suggest that we all be honest about the distractions in our lives, without judging ourselves, but also without perpetuating the negative affects those distractions have on us.

In a comparison mania world, we have a tendency to normalize bad habits because we see those same habits being perpetuated all around us. But, the reality is, that if we are squarely focused on what we deem important, we should be able to honestly evaluate how the distractions in our lives really affect how we show up in our own processes.

As I mentioned earlier, I struggled to build routines when it came to focusing on my purpose in life because I never had to do that. I never had to actually create routines for something I enjoyed, because I was typically good at the things that I chose to do. But when it came to honing my craft and sharpening my mental iron, I struggled.

A large part of that struggle was rooted in the distractions that I overlooked, and made excuses for in my life. I needed these things, right? They were my outlets. They were my "therapy" when I needed them. Whether or not it was alcohol, partying, television, or traveling and eating, they all were requirements because I had defined them as necessary distractions. But let's be honest here, they were unhealthy behaviors that kept me stuck in my plan-B.

This topic on distractions is not about judging ourselves. It is solely focused on being honest about all that we allow into our minds and hearts. If we are honest with ourselves, we probably have more negative distractions in our lives than we would like to admit. And the idea of getting rid of those distractions brings about anxiety and a host of other emotions that we don't care to experience.

But, if we are in this experience to focus on our bold goals, eliminating the distractions that don't bring us value, that don't add value, is not chore, it is a requirement.

Start by writing out a list of the things that you turn to when you are feeling anything - good, bad or indifferent. Across from whatever those distractions are, write down the emotions that you feel when you turn to them. In a third column, right down whether it adds value to your life. If the answer is yes, write down what type of value it adds. If the answer is no, go ahead and scratch it off. Be mindful, if something doesn't add value, that doesn't mean that it is a horrible thing. This exercise is to get you laser focused on what HAS value, so that you can make informed decisions on how to persist forward.

At this point you are a grownup in the room and you can make your own choices. But making the choice means that you need to understand the full scope of the circumstance. You make the choice, you eliminate distractions that don't add value, and you focus on what the priority is at hand.

Prioritize self-care

Whether on social media or just reading articles about life and leadership, self-care often is a topic that frequently is debated. But self-care is not just a buzz term that we should throw around because it sounds good and feels good. Self-care is not only essential to our success, it's foundational in how we craft healthy lives.

In the middle of my career transition into leadership development, I was so dedicated to learning and doing, I was treating my body like a punching bag. Literally, I was not sleeping enough, I was not eating well, and I was still drinking and doing drugs. My self-care meter was at an all time low, even as I was trying to care for others.

You don't have to be in the leadership development business to know that self-care is a priority in anyone's life. If you're treating your body, your temple, like a punching bag, how do you expect to care for anyone else? Yes, you can definitely care for people and not treat yourself well. But why would you want to do that? Why would you want to serve at half capacity when you could serve at full capacity? The entire idea of burn out comes from not focusing on self-care, while stretching yourself for others.

I am as guilty as the next person when it comes to being so wrapped up in my own stuff, that I have beat my body up, consciously and subconsciously. The question comes down to do you want to be show up partially, or do you want to show up as your whole self and have a more impactful influence?

If you choose the latter, then my suggestion is that you begin to take a hard look at your thoughts, habits, and behaviors. Go back to your distractions and figure out what adds value and what detracts from you. Because whatever is adding value can be positioned as a positive contribution to your life.

Start small and build your way up. Depending on where you are starting from will ultimately determine "how" you begin the process of constructing your self-care routine. What I recognized in my own experience was I needed to set micro wins and, in this case, micro steps, in order to begin caring for myself in a manner that revealed results for me and for those in my care.

7. FAITH-WORKS

Unshakable belief: Faith over Fear

. . . .

Faith without works is dead. And faith, works - always has, always will. This chapter isn't about religion. But it is about the necessary faith that it takes to achieve your plan-A in life; to conquer your worst fears, and to see your big vision come to life. If you are a believer in a higher power at all, then you can relate to this chapter. If not, I still hope you continue to read.

There are many types of faith that we can lean on in our lives. But in my life, I've always started with my spiritual faith. Now, everyone does not have the same type of spiritual faith. And to me this is quite OK. But what I do understand is that we all are here, created by a greater being. And for me, that means that we must have faith in a higher power in order to fully see the manifestations of our purpose.

Faith doesn't begin with our "needs". Faith begins with a commitment to believing in something, or someone, greater than self. And we must be able to fully embrace that there is so much in life that we simply have no control over; that's when faith is at its best.

Again, all of us don't have the same faith, nor should we. That's what makes us so unique as a species. Whatever your faith may be, no matter how devout or otherwise, *faith without works is dead.* The question many of us have is, *how do we stay rooted in our faith, while seeking to fulfill extraordinary purpose?*

I've been asked on more than one occasion, what should one do when life doesn't unfold like one imagined? What happens when one's faith seems to not be "working" on behalf of one's vision? It's a tough and pretty complex question. But there are some fairly sensible, yet dynamic answers.

Faith in yourself

- Win in your thoughts - *what happens in your mind will show up in your life, whether you want it to or not.*

- Be committed in your beliefs - *if you treat your faith as if it can be turned on and off like a faucet, you will end up always craving a drink of water. But if water your faith, thoughtfully, consistently, and with gratitude, your faith will keep you.*

- Give yourself grace - *forgive yourself, love yourself, and honor yourself.*

Win in your thoughts, first

What does it matter to have faith, without having faith in yourself? Are they independent of one another? Can one exist without the other? How about faith, period, is not relegated to the spiritual context. Faith in yourself is in fact a necessary component of living a life of purpose. How you think, how you win in your thoughts, projects the faith you have in yourself and your abilities to conquer all obstacles placed in front of you.

When I was younger I remember my sport coaches would always talk to us about the mental part of the game. No matter if it was baseball, tennis, or basketball, they would always talk to us about having our head in the game. I recall it like it was yesterday, because it was literally the same speech every single time - *Get your head in the game, it's mental.*

And now as we tackle these big goals that we have in front of us, the way we win in our thoughts, the way we get our head in the game, is essential to us being able to persevere. There are zero people living today that only win in their actions. We must always win in our thoughts, first. Because thoughts ultimately become habits, and habits are what we consistently do.

The questions we should ask ourselves: What have I accomplished in life that has challenged me to win in my thoughts? How did that make me feel? How did I do it? What pushed me to get there?

Winning in one's thoughts is not as easy or as difficult as one may believe. It is just as complex or simple as we allow ourselves to understand it. But if everything that was worth having in life was easy, then there wouldn't exist champions and runner-ups. Don't get me wrong, life is more than just winning and losing. But, to be clear, winning is what we are trying to accomplish; no matter if it's in sports, school, or in life. Winning - winning in our thoughts, is in fact the cornerstone of persisting to grasp the blessing of our plan A.

Imagine if you lived in a world that you knew what would happen every single moment of the day. Would you be able to win in your thoughts then? Would that be easier? If so, then I'm sorry, but that's not how life works. But, what if when you wake up every day, you know for certain that you have the power to set the tone for what is about to happen - that's where faith begins.

Be committed in your beliefs

Being committed in your beliefs is as serious as believing in someone you love. Whether it be a spouse, child, or family member, your beliefs are just as important, but just in a different way. If someone were to ask you, what do you believe in, what would you say? Do you automatically assume that they are referencing a spiritual belief or a personal belief system? What comes to mind immediately when you hear that type of question?

For many people, speaking about what they believe in spiritually or even personally, can be very intimidating and, in many ways, perplexing. When we share our belief system, we are opening ourselves up in a vulnerable state, that if given the choice, many of us would choose to not do so. But for this moment, let's set aside distinguishing between beliefs of a spiritual nature and those of a personal nature. Let's just address being committed in our beliefs.

Are you committed in your beliefs? I know this can sound like a loaded question, but it is very simple. The question is about your commitment in the belief that you have about who you are, what you do, and where you want to go in life. Are you committed? Well, some people may ask, "What if I don't have any specific beliefs?" My response to that is think about what you may believe in, or what you want to believe in, and try starting there.

But those of us who do have beliefs, those of us who do espouse to believe in something specific, whether it be spiritual, or otherwise, we need to ask ourselves this question. Are we committed? Being committed in one's beliefs is essential to being equipped with the necessary mindset to push through towards your most audacious goals in life. And that would certainly include accomplishing your plan-A.

If you find yourself asking the question *how do I know if I'm committed in my beliefs*, then you can take these steps. You should first be able to write down, in plain terms, what you believe in. What are your spiritual beliefs, your personal goals, your ethics and morals, whatever it may be? You must be able to outline how you actually exhibit your beliefs through your thoughts, words, and habits.

We must understand our behavior is an indication of what we believe in and what we consistently do. These habits support what we say we believe in, what we say we are committed to. And lastly, if you find a disconnect between what you say you believe in and what you see reflected in your habits and behaviors, then we must ask ourselves a different question.

That question must be, "Why don't my actions reflect my beliefs?" Often times, when we are trying to accomplish these big, bold goals of ours, we find ourselves in the zone. That zone has us doing work, moving forward, and going at a lightning speed every single hour of the day. And it can be easy to get lost in what we want for ourselves, and not recognize what we believe in. Belief is essential to doing anything that we say we want to do in this world.

I found myself vacillating every other week when I began my journey towards my plan-A. One week I was up and feeling great and thinking that this was the path that I was supposed to be on; and there was nothing else in this world that I should be doing but this work in helping people live better lives.

But then the following week I could be in a funk, and not feeling so certain about what I was doing. It felt like a roller coaster ride of emotions, and literally one can go stir crazy if you let the cycle of uncertainty take hold of you.

But what eventually happened for me was life changing. As I reflected on each of those previous years, I began to see real progress. I started to build up an armor, because I began to see my growth and my power. The key to this experience is not being certain, and yet persisting. Reverend T.D. Jakes says, and I'm para-phrasing, *if we were certain of everything that would happen in the world, then we would not need faith.* But because I was seeing the building blocks take shape, I was beginning to feel more confident, and because I was feeling more confident, I was able to truly become more *committed in my beliefs.*

I knew for sure that I was built on purpose, with purpose, and for purpose. I knew this in my soul. I knew it in every ounce of my body and being. But I too needed to look back over my shoulder and see the pain turn into purpose. We all need to see it. But many times when we are looking backwards, we only see failure. And if we only see what went wrong, we are blinded to the micros wins that actually happened. Remember the micro wins? All those missteps, all those losses, are actually our micro wins. And if we can just understand what those micro wins represent, we can then turn back around and look forward, and see what we are building towards; our plan-A.

Being committed in your beliefs is not simply about believing in yourself, or believing in your faith. Being committed in your beliefs takes work. It takes action. But more importantly, it takes understanding and perspective. In order to build up your armor in your belief system, you must do more than just believe. Take note of what has happened in your life, process it, write about it, evaluate it, and then craft your next move. If all we see in the world is what is not happening, then we totally will miss the experience of what is actually happening.

The journey to plan-A is not solely about an out-
t is keenly about the fundamentals of the process.
The reason why plan-B sucks is not only because it's somebody else's plan, but because it is a choice we make based
on an imaginary construct in our minds. It's the work that
we chose NOT to do in order to achieve our plan-A.

So much of being committed in our beliefs centers
on having faith in our path.   There are three things we
should hold firm to if we want to persevere through self-
doubt.   We must abandon our need for clarity, trust our
path is perfect, and prepare in presence. The idea that we
are going to know every single thing that's going to happen
in this journey of purpose and life fulfillment is really silly
and ridiculous. It just won't be that easy. It never has and it
never will be.

The distinction between those who are living a life
in plan-B and plan-C , and those of us who want to live our
plan-A, is very clear.   Plan-A people don't seek clarity on

what they can't control. Plan-A people focus on what they can control, and leave it to the universe to handle the rest.

Many people understand that the path is not perfect. What does that mean? Well, it means that everything that has happened, is happening, and will happen, is meant to happen. And I don't necessarily mean in the spiritual sense. I mean what happens is going to happen and we live with it, make do with it, and go with it.

We have all the time in the world to evaluate, but we don't have time to second guess. When we do the work; when we focus on the controllable; when we are committed in our beliefs, all that is supposed to happen will happen, without any interference from us.

Consequently, being committed in our beliefs means that we should prepare in presence. We must be present in the moments that matter the most to us. If we are seeking to achieve our plan-A, then we must be emotionally, mentally, spiritually, and physically present.

This is not about being perfect, this is not about having all the answers, but this is about being in the current moment. If we cannot be present in this moment, then this moment is not for us. Yes, it takes sacrifice. Yes, it takes will power. And yes, it takes a force of determination that many of us seek, but only a few of us will reach. That's the truth. The question is, how present are you for what matters most in your life?

Give yourself grace

I simply love this phrase - "give yourself grace". I didn't really understand what it meant until I began my business. When you are an entrepreneur, you find out things about yourself, your friends and family, and a host of other things in life that you never could have imagined. But more importantly, you find out how to forgive yourself - hopefully. I found out that me being my toughest critic wasn't really going to do me much good in the long run.

Yes, I will always be tough on myself; but I learned that being tough and being overly critical are two different behaviors. We just have to understand that being kind to ourselves is not a selfish act. Humans can be too hard on themselves; we see this in so many facets of our lives, from something as simple as not winning a card game to something as painful as a divorce. It seems that no matter the severity, we tend to be our harshest critics.

But if there is ever a time that we should be lifting ourselves up, it is in a journey of self discovery and self development. I mean, not knowing something is not the time when we should be beating ourselves up. We need "us". You need "you". I need "me". Get it? This is the time to give ourselves grace. What is grace? If you are a spiritual believer in the Bible, then you can receive that grace is unmerited mercy.

But even if you are not a follower of the Bible, grace is something that you should surely give to yourself at all times. Why? Because grace actually is saying to yourself, "I forgive me, I love me, and I honor me." Period. Grace is not about anything that you have done or not done, earned or not earned. It is given unconditionally. And so, we should give ourselves grace as much as possible, without one ounce of guilt.

If you find it hard to forgive yourself, ask yourself, "Why?" If you find it a challenge to love yourself, then ask yourself, "Why?" If you find yourself struggling to honor yourself, you must ask yourself, "Why?" These questions are not meant to shame you, or make you feel inferior. But we must ask them, because these are the questions that will allow us to shift our thoughts, and allow ourselves to forgive, love, and honor ourselves with grace.

Faith over Fear

Unfortunately, or fortunately, depending on how one wants to view it, fear is a noun and a verb in the dictionary. Why is it that fear can become so paralyzing? What makes fear turn from a noun into a verb? It's all in our heads, and in our hearts too! Fear is that crazy topic that we all talk about, hear about, and laugh about, but I don't know anyone that has the answers to what fear really is. But I have heard some fairly good explanations recently. I'm not here to talk about the right and wrong way to discuss failure. However, I am here to share with you why fear is fuel, and fuel gives us the ability to go far if we know how to use it.

What fear is/isn't

Fear is real; it's not good or bad, and it is definitely not fatal. If you think for one moment that crossing a street with moving cars doesn't put fear in one's entire body, then you are fooling yourself. Fear is natural, normal, and required. So this idea that fear is imaginary is a made up piece of crap. Fear is real. Now that we have gotten out of the way, let's outline what fear is and what fear is not.

Fear isn't good or bad. Fear is actually what you allow it to be; it is what we make it. Crossing the street with moving cars, jumping out of a plane without a parachute, or doing anything that may harm us or someone else, requires fear. That fear, is fear we need. If you want to define it as good, be my guest. I just define it as a necessity.

The need to define everything by either being good or bad can be a personal constraint. In doing so, we can trivialize and or diminish the actual existence of something or someone. Fear, itself, is a natural emotion. But how we use it, or how we allow it to use us, becomes the most important question at hand. Fear is not fatal if we use it correctly. Just like any other emotion, if we actually allow ourselves to feel the emotion in a manner in which informs us, empowers us, and activates us, then we are using fear for fuel.

Fear is the natural emotion that is instructive in all times and ways. I simply love fear. Because fear lets me know that I'm on the right path to something. Now, what that something is, is the question. It may be stopping something or starting something. But it is an indicator, and because it indicates something, I love it. Who doesn't want an indicator in their life's journey? Who doesn't want something to pop up every single time something is about to happen? I do! And you should too. Fear is the most instructive, exhilarating, and useful emotion that we can feel.

I recall being younger and learning a poem that included a stanza that cited "Fear is a mind killer, we must learn to conquer fear and overcome it." And to some degree that stanza has specks of truth in it. But fear only kills the mind if we allow it to. And we don't need to conquer or overcome fear, we simply need to use fear.

Question: How do we use fear? We should use fear in three ways - to take our temperature, to focus on what matters, and to be extraordinary. So what does it mean to take one's temperature? Simply put, when we take our temperature we find out what is really happening inside of us. So when we take our temperature in life, we find out where we actually are in our journey. Fear does that for us. Fear steps in and challenges us to take our temperature in the most uncomfortable places. These are the places that we think we should be in, but we have self-doubt and mis-givings about how we arrived here, if we should be here, and begin to relive our imposter syndrome.

Fear forces us to focus on what matters. Many of us choose to disregard fear, or even stop in our journey and question what fear really means. At minimum, fear should push us to focus on what we feel matters the most in life. I like to think of fear giving us a strong nudge- just letting us know that we will have to do more, show up more, and give more in order to get to where we say we want to be. If it's truly plan-A that we want, then we have to stop living in fear - living in plan-B.

But what I love most about fear is that it forces us to be extraordinary. Now what does that mean? It means exactly what it says. Fear drives each of us to literally make a choice to either be average or extraordinary. Look, there's nothing wrong with average. Many of us fall into the category of average in much of what we do in life. But if we want to be extraordinary in our purpose, fear will get us there. But we must use fear as fuel to be extraordinary. When people look at sports and business icons, we find that they all were pushed to the limits in fear, and it drove them to be extraordinary.

I've said it many times before, and I'll say it again here. Average is given, greatness is earned. If we do not use fear as fuel, we miss the greatest opportunity to live in our plan-A, to be extraordinary, and to fulfill the purpose that we have in our lives. There is no greater loss than to succumb to fear. Please, whatever you do, do not let fear off the hook. Use it, or it will use you!

8. BE YOUR #1 FAN

Champion YOUR greatness

. . . .

There's you, and then there is everyone else. There is literally not one person in the world that looks like you, thinks like you, or compares to you. No one will ever see your vision as you see it. There is no one in the world who will be as passionate, committed, or determined to do what YOU want to accomplish in your life. You are not only the person who is writing your story, you are the movie director, the producer, and if you really want to be honest with yourself, you are actually the audience. Simply put, if you do not champion your greatness, no one will. If you are not your number one fan, nobody will be.

As early as we can remember, we all looked to someone or some thing for confirmation and affirmation. Parents, grandparents, loved ones, you name it, we looked for it. When we were babies, we looked up into the eyes of whomever was looking back at us and we wanted affirmations. We wanted to be affirmed that we were all what we thought we should be. As we grew up in the world, we did not shy away from needing more of these affirmations. The more we received, the more we required. It's as if we never knew of any other way to exist. And indeed, the affirmations only allow us to exist, not to live.

When I was growing up as a little boy, my mother didn't mix words. She let me know that I could do anything that I put my mind to. I held firm to that belief, even though later on in life I really understood what she was saying to me was much deeper. She was sharing with me the sentiment of believing in myself, and that all things are possible. That sentiment is something that I hold dear in my heart being till this day. I became keenly aware of why

r number one fan is not just a cute little term that

od and feels good in a speech or a song. Because

at some point in life, all the people that love us, all the people that care about us, all the people who truly do believe in us, will be detached from our vision, because our vision is not for them to see.

So what happens when our vision can't be seen by anyone else? Not even our closest friends and love ones can see it. Not even those who have tracked the journey with us can see it. What happens with a vision that is in our hearts and minds that can only can been by us? Who is your number one fan in that moment? Who believes in you?

Now if you are a spiritual believer like I am, you know that there is a God on high and that we are never alone. And if you understand that you are never alone, you understand that you being your number one fan doesn't mean you are your only fan. Because when there is no one that can see your vision, you can trust that God not only sees your vision, God planted your vision. And we don't have to have the same belief system to understand this. But the idea of understanding why plan-B sucks, is rooted in fundamentally knowing that there is a higher power that guides the universe.

I meet people everywhere I go and everywhere I speak that have *extraordinary* right there in front of them. But they're looking for someone to be their number one fan; they're looking for the confirmations and affirmations that they received all throughout their lives, and now there is silence. But remember, there is power in silence, there is growth in that aloneness. What does it mean to have silence around you? It doesn't mean that we are on the wrong path, it does not mean that no one believes in us; it means that something is working. It means that something is being transformed, *and if we refuse to take action, then we are acquiescing our extraordinary for average.*

If I have to put my finger on it and give you one good reason why you must be your number one fan, it's because you don't get to plan-A without it. That's it. Nobody reaches their plan-A by waiting on someone else or something else to confirm them and affirm their purpose. Life simply doesn't work that way. Plan-B sucks because we are waiting on someone else to tell us that it's time to step into our extraordinary. Plan-B sucks because we are waiting for the right moment, the right gesture, the right time and place where we can step into our greatness without being uncomfortable.

The moral of the story is: getting to plan-A is super uncomfortable, it's lonely as hell, it's frustrating, it's up and down, it's fear and faith, it's sad and happy, it's all the things that you would not desire in a life of average. But for a life of extraordinary, you would welcome it in a heartbeat. So go ahead, live in your plan-A.

Why? Because plan-B sucks!

ABOUT THE AUTHOR

Glenn Thomas is the founder and Chief Heart Officer of Heart Work Leadership Group, a firm that has had the honor of serving organizations and leaders for over seven years. Glenn has served in senior leadership roles for corporate, government and nonprofit organizations for over twenty years, and dedicates his time and research on uncovering what leaders need to fully excel in both their lives and careers. Glenn is a keynote speaker, leadership practitioner, and author of Heart Work: 19 Expressions of Heart-Centered Leaders. Highlighting principles of life and leadership, *Heart Work* charges leaders to be vulnerable and courageous in order to live, love, and lead from the inside-out.

To book Glenn for keynotes and training events:
info@weinspirepeople.com
support@glennathomas.com
(833) 999-LEAD

Made in the USA
Monee, IL
11 May 2021